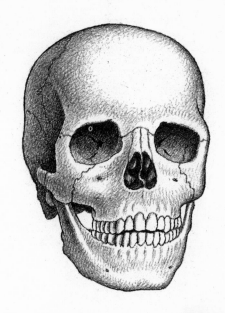

BONES
HERBERT S. ZIM

illustrated by RENÉ MARTIN

William Morrow and Company New York

Second printing, September 1970

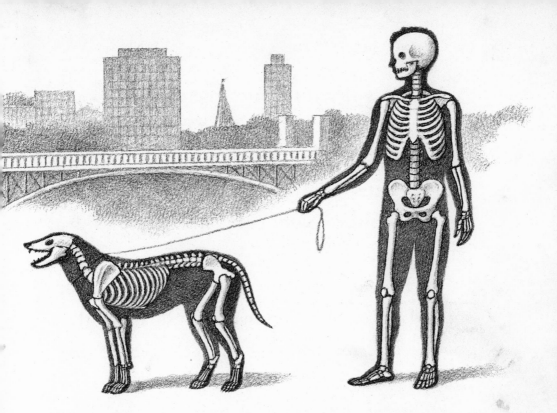

If you had X-ray eyes and could look
through skin and muscles, you would see
all people and many animals in the form of
living skeletons. You would see that a skeleton of bones is as neatly planned as a
bridge or satellite. Bones make it possible
for fish to swim, birds to fly, and human
beings to run, jump, and walk erectly.

Animals lived before there were bones, however. Some 400 million years ago, the seas were full of simple creatures, like crinoids, tetracorals, brachiopods, eurypteroids, and trilobites. None of those animals had any bones.

A hundred million years later bones appeared in fishlike animals. Animals with a bony skeleton had a better chance to live, mainly because they could move faster. As millions of years slipped by, more and more kinds of backboned animals were seen. A hundred million years ago, they were already common on land, in the sea, and in the air.

OSTRACODERMS,
FISHLIKE ANIMALS WITH BONES
300 million years ago

pteraspid

Thelodus

Hemicyclaspis

BACKBONED ANIMALS
100 million years ago

Archaeopteryx

tyrannosaur

brontosaur

Scientists do not know exactly how or when the first bones developed. Possibly they first formed in small fresh-water swimming animals. With a central column of bones to support their muscles, these animals could swim better, catch more food, and escape more enemies. All animals that have developed this central column, or backbone, are called vertebrates.

pterodactyl

BACKBONED ANIMALS
100 million years ago

plesiosaur

archelon

Vertebrates are the most important animals on earth. They are the fishes, amphibians (frogs and their kin), reptiles (snakes, turtles, and lizards), birds, and mammals. This last great group ranges from shrews that weigh less than a dime to great whales weighing well over 100 tons. All of these vertebrates have skeletons of bone, and all are built pretty much on the same plan.

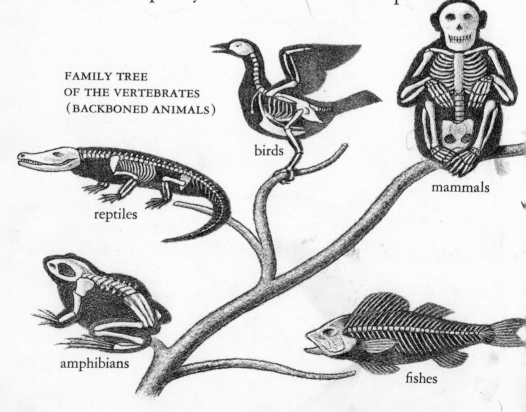

FAMILY TREE
OF THE VERTEBRATES
(BACKBONED ANIMALS)

birds

mammals

reptiles

amphibians

fishes

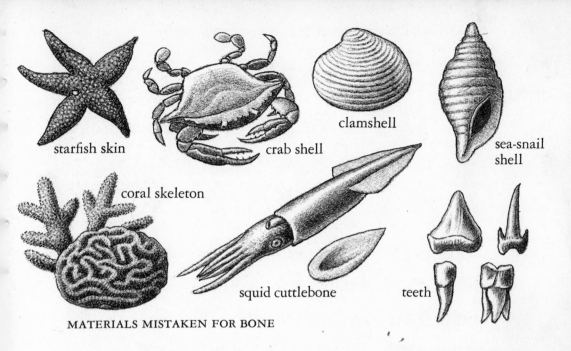

starfish skin

crab shell

clamshell

sea-snail
shell

coral skeleton

squid cuttlebone

teeth

MATERIALS MISTAKEN FOR BONE

But even today many animals get along
quite well without bones. Sea snails and
clams have a hard shell, but it is not bone.
Starfish and sea urchins are encased in armor,
some with moveable spines, but these cover-
ings are not made of bone. Coral animals
have a "skeleton," but it is not made of
bone. The hard, white rod, called cuttlebone,
inside the squid is not bone either. In fact,
what is bone?

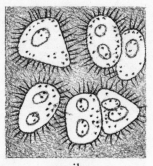 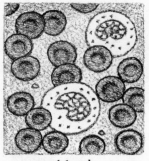 

cartilage   blood   bone

Bone is one of the tissues of the vertebrate body. Tissues are groups of similar cells (and materials between the cells) that do the same work in the body. Bone is one kind of connective tissue. Other kinds include blood, fat, fibrous tissue (as tendons), and cartilage.

Your growth, inch by inch, is mainly the result of your bones growing longer. This growth depends, in part, on who your parents are. It depends on body chemicals like vitamins and hormones. It depends also on the foods you eat. All these factors fix the pattern of how fast you grow and how much.

The bones of people are very much like the bones of other vertebrates. All are far from bone dry. About one quarter of living bone is water. This proportion varies with the kind of bone. About one third is organic. Organic chemicals contain the element carbon and often hydrogen, oxygen, nitrogen, sulfur, and phosphorus. This organic matter in bones includes various kinds of living bone cells, blood and blood vessels, fats, and several materials somewhat like gelatin. The most important of them are fibers of collagen.

COLLAGEN FIBERS SEEN THROUGH AN ELECTRON MICROSCOPE

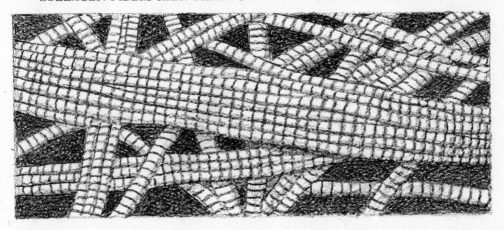

The rest of the bone is made of inorganic or mineral substances. They are simpler chemicals that are deposited as crystals in bone or dissolved in bone tissue.

The most common mineral in bone is calcium phosphate. This chemical is made of three elements: calcium, phosphorus, and oxygen. A very similar combination in rocks forms the mineral apatite, well-known for its blue, green, and yellow crystals. Another mineral in bone is calcium carbonate, the chemical that also forms seashells and coral. In addition, bone contains some magnesium chemicals and other minor minerals.

TWO MINERALS FOUND IN BONE

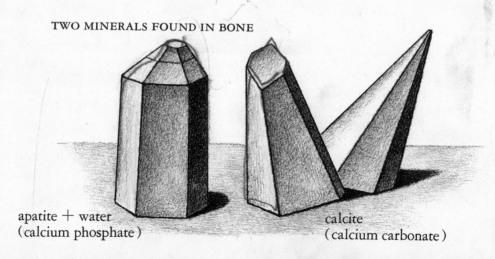

apatite + water
(calcium phosphate)

calcite
(calcium carbonate)

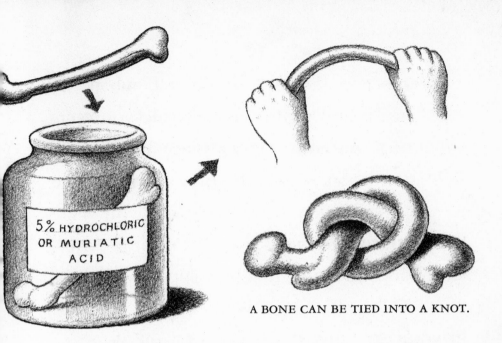

A BONE CAN BE TIED INTO A KNOT.

Minerals give bone their strength and hardness. You can see this fact for yourself if you save the leg bone of a chicken or turkey and clean off all the meat. Put the bone in a jar and cover it with a weak acid. Sometimes strong vinegar will do. In a week or two the acid will dissolve much of the mineral in the bone. Remove the bone and bend it. It will curve like a piece of rubber. You can even tie a knot in a long bone.

You began life as a single cell, which divided again and again. For a while you were an animal without a backbone. But special cells that soon would become bone started to develop. Seven months before you were born, your bones were already forming. Arms, legs, backbone, and ribs first appeared as cells of cartilage. Cartilage is the softer material in your ears and at the end of your nose.

BONES FORMING BEFORE BIRTH
(enlarged about 4 times)

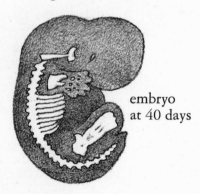

embryo
at 40 days

At 40 days
the bone pattern
can be seen.
At 60 days
bones are formed
and growing.

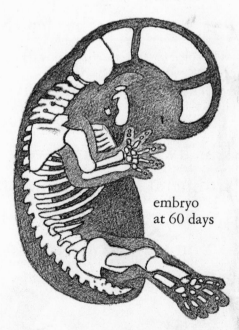

embryo
at 60 days

Slowly the cartilage cells are replaced by bone cells, which begin to deposit minerals. In short bones, like those of your wrists, the change begins at the center and moves toward the ends. In long bones, like those of your arms and legs, the change starts at the middle and at both ends as well. These bones harden from the center toward the ends and from the ends toward the center.

Flat bones, like those of your skull and shoulder blades, do not form from cartilage. Flat bones form from a membrane. They become hard and smooth at the surface, but remain softer and spongier inside.

HARDENING OF THIGHBONE (FEMUR)

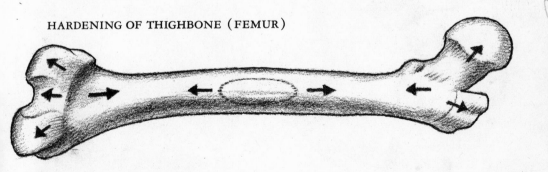

The hardening of bone is a slow process. At the time a baby is born, it is far from complete. A baby's bones are soft and are still mainly cartilage. The flat bones of the skull are not complete either. There are gaps between the bones, leaving about six soft spots, or fontanels. One large fontanel at the top of the baby's head can be felt easily. The skull bones grow and close the fontanel by the time the baby is a year and a half old.

TOP OF SKULL

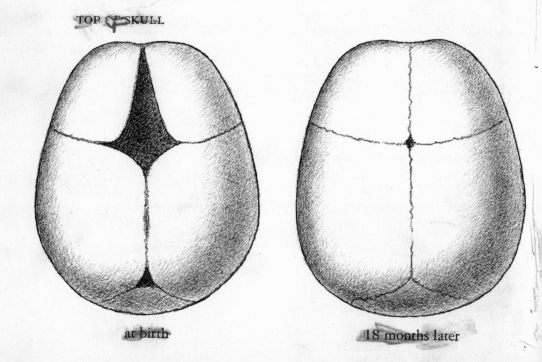

at birth   18 months later

At birth there is bone in a baby's arms and legs. But its wrists still are made of cartilage. Slowly they change and harden. A doctor looking at an X ray of a boy's hand can tell how old he is. When young, a child's backbone, or vertebral column, has 33 bones. But as he becomes an adult, the four bones at the very end (the tailbones) fuse together into one. The next five bones above also fuse together so that nine bones become two.

Bones of arms and legs grow longer and sturdier till a person is about 17 or 18. By that time, most people have reached their full height. But bone growth (mainly hardening) continues for another ten years or so.

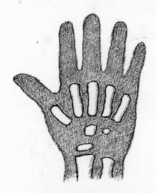

X RAYS SHOW
HOW WRISTBONES
FORM AND GROW
IN CHILDREN.

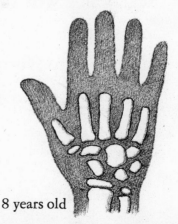

3 years old   8 years old

whole-wheat bread · almonds · eggs · scallops · milk · ice cream · cheese · cabbage

The growth of bone depends on the minerals that are in food, on Vitamin D, and, to some extent, on Vitamin C. Dairy foods that most of us eat, such as milk, cheese, and ice cream, usually contain ample calcium, phosphorus, and vitamins. If very young children do not get enough calcium, phosphorus, or Vitamin D for a long time, their leg bones will soften and may grow bent and misshapen. Then they have rickets, once a disease of poverty. Sunlight helps in forming Vitamin D and so prevents rickets.

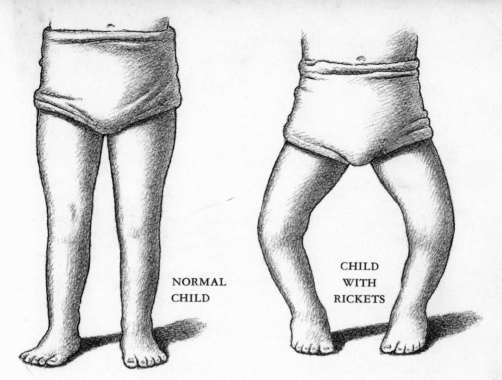

NORMAL CHILD

CHILD WITH RICKETS

Dissolved calcium and phosphorus needed for bone growth are circulated by the blood. But the control of the amount of these two chemicals in the blood rests with two pairs of small glands in the throat, just under the chin. These parathyroid glands are each about the size of a pea. They lie inside or just next to a larger gland, the thyroid, which helps the body get energy from food.

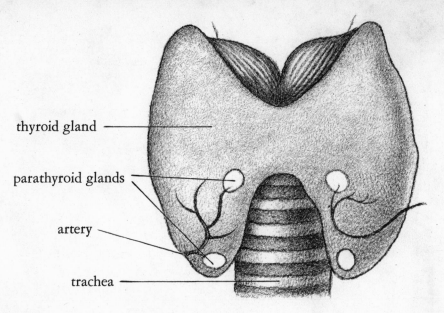

thyroid gland

parathyroid glands

artery

trachea

The chemicals from these glands balance calcium and phosphorus in the blood. Other body chemicals—vitamins, enzymes, and hormones—also have an effect on bone growth.

After all your bones have grown, you have a skeleton of 206 bones that will serve you the rest of your life. An extra bone or two may show up in your kneecap or along skull joints, but they hardly count. Here you are without your skin and flesh, and here are the different bones of your body.

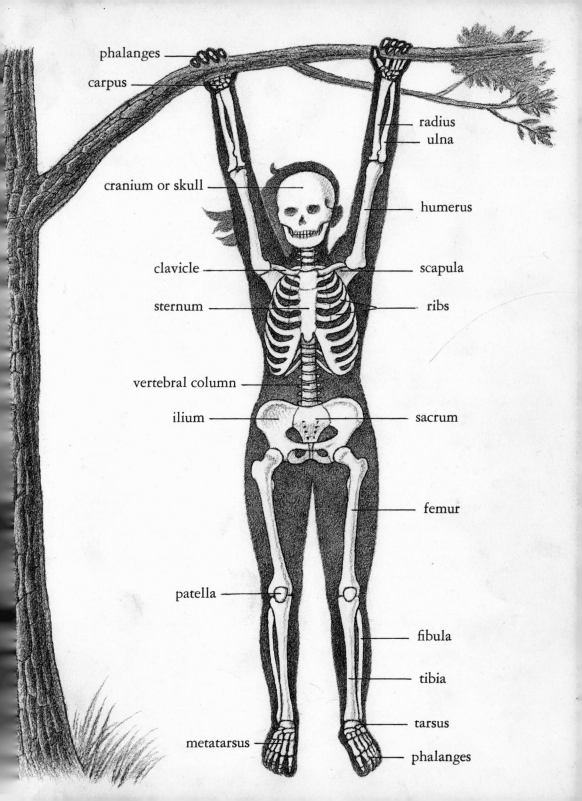

phalanges

carpus

radius

ulna

cranium or skull

humerus

clavicle

scapula

sternum

ribs

vertebral column

ilium

sacrum

femur

patella

fibula

tibia

tarsus

metatarsus

phalanges

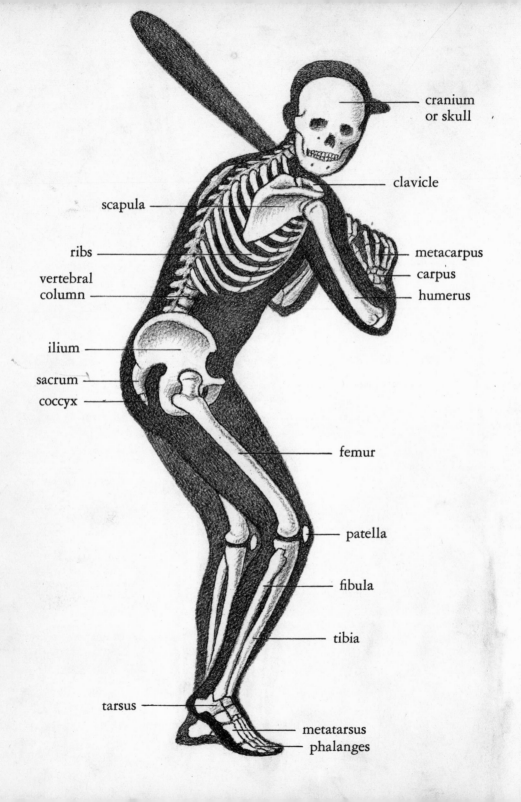

cranium
or skull

clavicle

scapula

ribs

metacarpus

carpus

vertebral
column

humerus

ilium

sacrum

coccyx

femur

patella

fibula

tibia

tarsus

metatarsus

phalanges

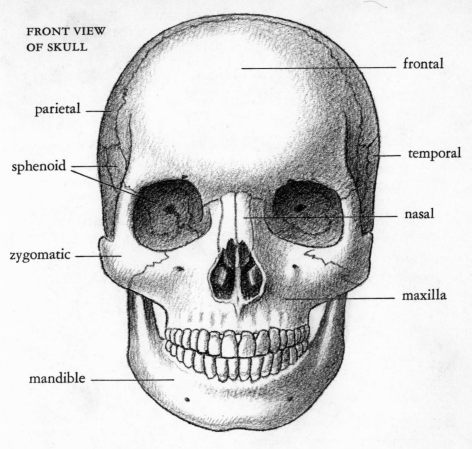

FRONT VIEW
OF SKULL

frontal

parietal

sphenoid

temporal

nasal

zygomatic

maxilla

mandible

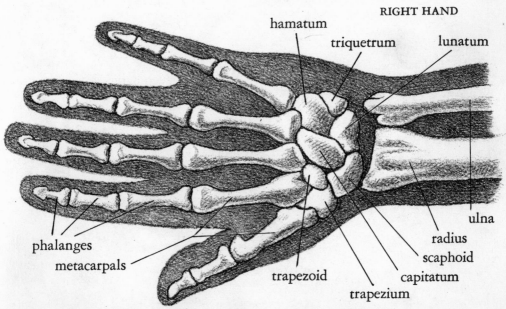

RIGHT HAND

hamatum

triquetrum

lunatum

phalanges

metacarpals

trapezoid

trapezium

capitatum

scaphoid

radius

ulna

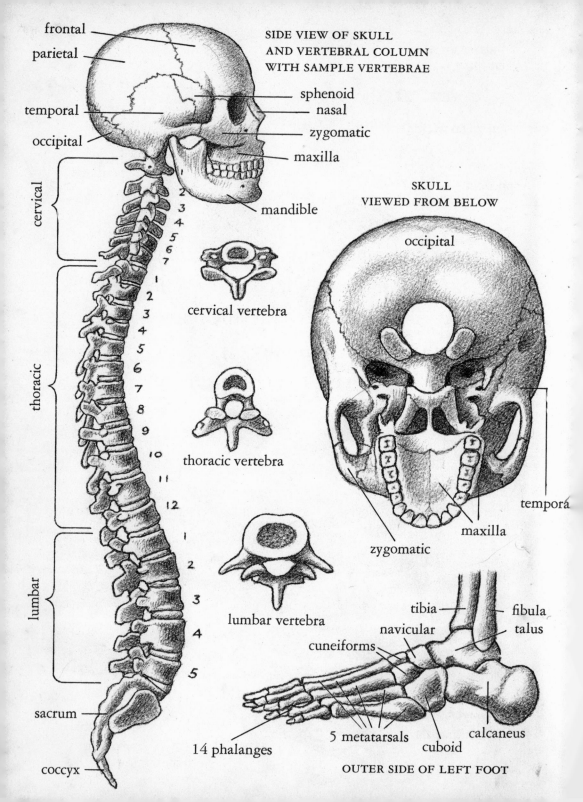

frontal

parietal

SIDE VIEW OF SKULL
AND VERTEBRAL COLUMN
WITH SAMPLE VERTEBRAE

temporal

sphenoid

nasal

occipital

zygomatic

maxilla

cervical

mandible

SKULL
VIEWED FROM BELOW

occipital

2
3
4
5
6
7

cervical vertebra

1
2
3
4
5
6
7
8
9
10
11
12

thoracic

thoracic vertebra

temporal

maxilla

zygomatic

1
2
3
4
5

lumbar

lumbar vertebra

tibia

fibula

navicular

talus

cuneiforms

sacrum

14 phalanges

5 metatarsals

cuboid

calcaneus

coccyx

OUTER SIDE OF LEFT FOOT

In general, the bones of the body fall into four main groups. Long bones have a slight curve, which helps them support a load better than if they were perfectly straight. The ends of the shafts are swollen and made of softer, spongier bone with a thin, hard cover. Here muscles, which move arms and legs, are attached. Most of the movements that are fun—the running, jumping, and throwing—make use of your long bones.

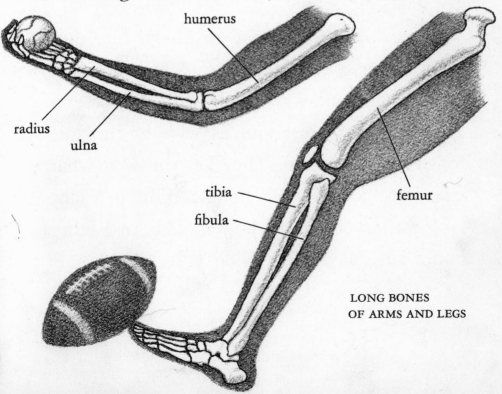

humerus

radius

ulna

tibia

fibula

femur

**LONG BONES
OF ARMS AND LEGS**

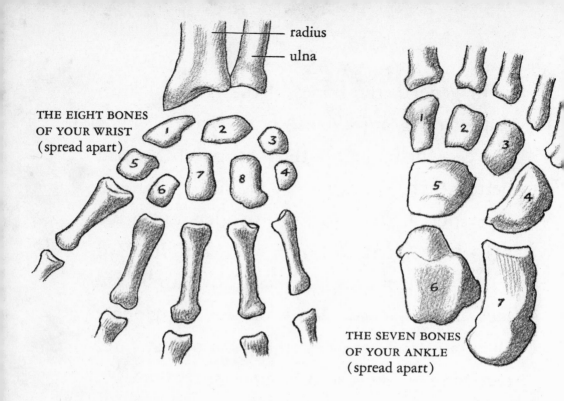

radius
ulna

THE EIGHT BONES
OF YOUR WRIST
(spread apart)

THE SEVEN BONES
OF YOUR ANKLE
(spread apart)

Some long bones may be short, but they always have a distinct shaft. What the anatomist, who studies the body, calls short bones are those that are about as wide as they are long—almost square. They are the somewhat irregular spongy wrist bones (eight in each) and the seven ankle bones. The two knee bones are called short bones also.

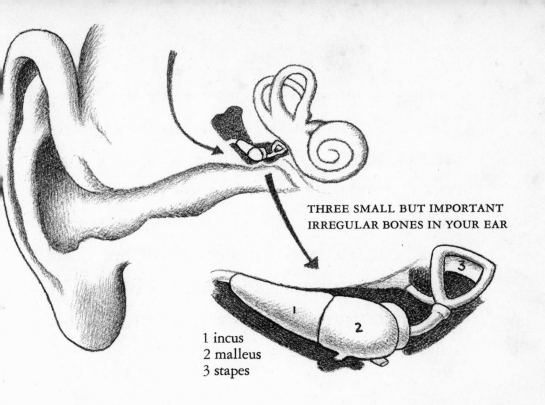

THREE SMALL BUT IMPORTANT
IRREGULAR BONES IN YOUR EAR

1 incus
2 malleus
3 stapes

Some long bones are short and most short bones are irregular. The name of the third group of bones, however, matches their shape. The irregular bones are really irregular. They include the 33 vertebrae in your backbone, the three little bones in each ear, and some of the bones that make up your face. This is a really mixed-up group of bones.

The last group of bones are the flat bones. They are a bit curved rather than flat. Ribs are flat bones, although they look like long bones at first glance. Most of the bones of your skull, your shoulder blades, and your breastbone are also flat bones. All are quite hard at the surface and spongy within. The next time you eat spareribs you can see what a flat bone is like.

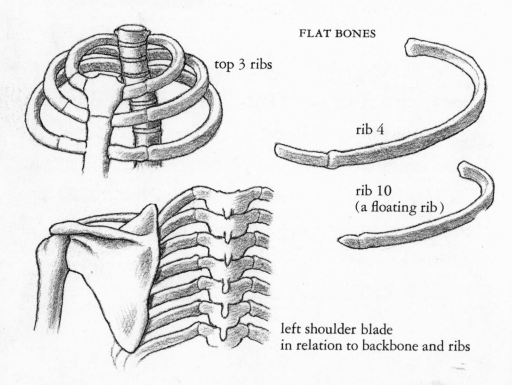

FLAT BONES

top 3 ribs

rib 4

rib 10
(a floating rib)

left shoulder blade
in relation to backbone and ribs

To classify bones, you must study and understand each one. Each grows in its own special way and each has a special job in the body. Doctors study the skeleton in great detail. It *is* the framework of the body, and the medical student begins his study of anatomy with it. He must learn every single bone. Doctors know that part of being well depends on how people use their skeleton.

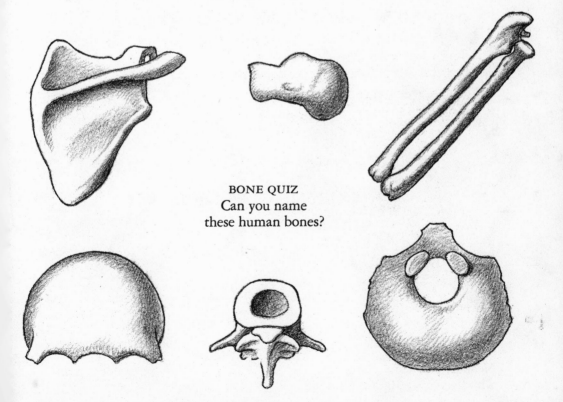

BONE QUIZ
Can you name
these human bones?

Archeologists, who dig up ruins and study ancient man, are even more interested in bones. All we know about very early man has been learned from things he made and from the few bones of his skeleton that have been found. Every detail of these old bones is studied and every part is compared to bones of people living today.

Most bones have ridges, knobs, and raised parts to which muscles are attached. Experts

SKULLS OF TWO KINDS OF MEN
Compare eye ridges, teeth, jaws, and size of skull.

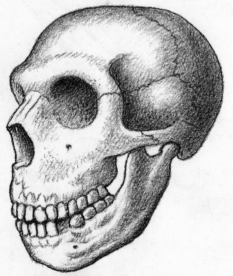

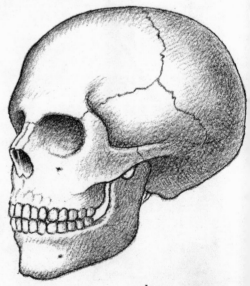

Neanderthal man,
who lived over 50,000 years ago

modern man

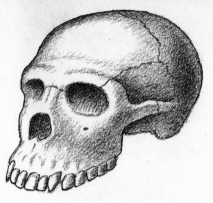

SKULL AND RESTORATION
OF MANLIKE APE
(AUSTRALOPITHECUS)

know every muscle and how it forms the
flesh over every bone. If these ridges and
knobs on bones are large, they probably sup-
ported a larger muscle. So a skilled student
of bones can make a good guess about the
looks of a man who lived long ago, if he
finds enough skull bones. He can tell if his
subject had a high or low forehead or had
ridges over his eyes. He can estimate the
size of the jaw, the thickness of the neck,
and the structure of nose, cheeks, or chin.

PROCONSUL,
which lived about
20 million years ago,
had both apelike
and manlike features.

The study of bones tells scientists that man could not possibly have descended from monkeys. It does show that man and the great apes, like the gorilla and chimpanzee, are closely related. They both may have come from the same ancestors ten million or more years ago. The study of skulls and hip bones suggests that this ancient ancestor was able to walk upright and perhaps think.

An expert often can distinguish the bones of a man, woman, or child. Size plays a part. Children's bones are not only smaller, they show less hardening. There may be gaps between them, and they may not be complete. The bones of a woman are usually smaller and more delicate than those of a man. Furthermore, the hips (pelvis) of a woman are wider in every direction than those of a man; the openings are larger and more oval. This difference helps a woman carry a baby before birth and makes the baby's birth easier.

MALE PELVIS

FEMALE PELVIS

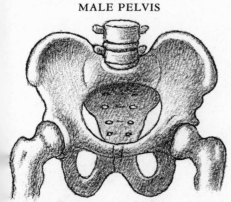

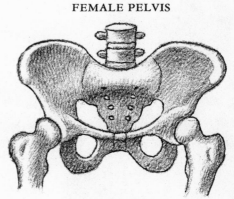

narrow and high

wide and shallow

Only the shaded bones have been found.

BRONTOSAUR SKELETON

Animal bones also yield much information. Bones of dinosaurs 200 million years old have been dug up, and from them the whole animal has been reconstructed even though a good many bones are missing.

BRONTOSAUR
restored from a study of its bones

Old bones tell us the story of our past, but our living bones are the ones that we use every day. Your bones are all alive and will keep living until you yourself die. They are just as much alive as your blood, muscles, skin, and brain. Living bones support your body and make it possible for you to move and lift things. In addition, the marrow of your bone makes red blood cells. Bones protect delicate parts of your body. Skull bones wrap around and protect your brain. Ribs form a strong cage around your lungs.

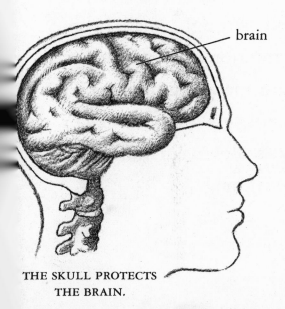

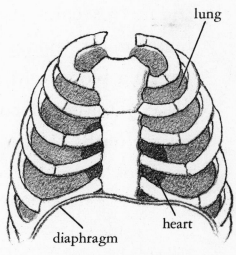

brain

lung

diaphragm

heart

**THE SKULL PROTECTS
THE BRAIN.**

**THE RIBS PROTECT
THE LUNGS AND HEART.**

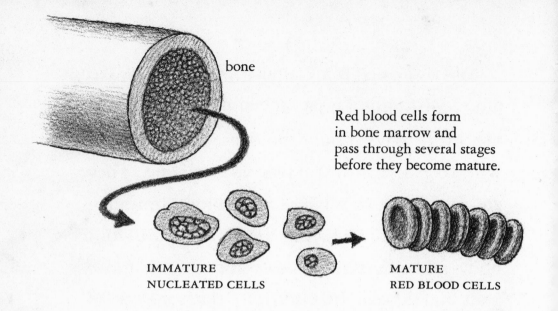

bone

Red blood cells form
in bone marrow and
pass through several stages
before they become mature.

IMMATURE
NUCLEATED CELLS

MATURE
RED BLOOD CELLS

Living bone is hard to imagine. Your muscles move; your eyes see; your brain thinks. But bones do not seem to be doing anything. Yet they are alive. Blood vessels and nerves enter them through small openings. In the spongy interior of some bones, new red blood cells are made, enough to replace your blood completely every three or four months. If your bones were not alive, you would not live very long.

Your living bones take food from the blood and give waste chemicals to it just like all other living cells. And like the other cells of your body, bone cells are formed, live, die, and are replaced by new cells. The balance between tearing down and building up bone is a very delicate one. When a person is young, building up goes on faster than breaking down. But even then, the balance is carefully controlled.

DIFFERENT RATES OF GROWTH AT DIFFERENT AGES
Before birth the bones of the skull grow most rapidly.
Later the limbs grow faster.
Each part of the body has its own growth pattern.

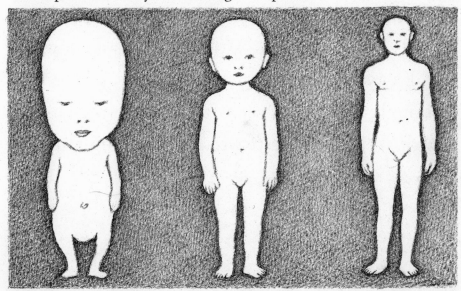

before birth   baby   adult

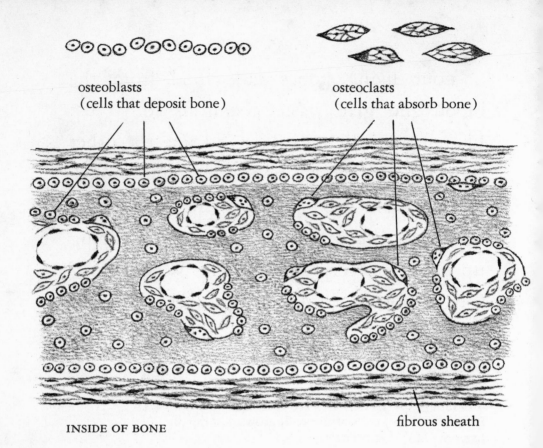

osteoblasts
(cells that deposit bone)

osteoclasts
(cells that absorb bone)

INSIDE OF BONE

fibrous sheath

The cells that produce bone are of two kinds—a type that dissolves, or tears down, and a type that deposits, or builds up. Oddly enough, these cells seem to be able to change back and forth—destroyers at one time, builders at another.

Within the bones of your arm or ribs at this very moment bone cells are gradually breaking down the bone. Chemicals or enzymes from these cells dissolve the bone and release the dissolved calcium. This slow work goes on in only one part of a bone at a time. In this area, holes the size of a pinhead develop. Then, before the bone is really weakened or damaged, the bone cells change jobs or new cells come in and begin to deposit fresh bone. So your bones are constantly being replaced and rebuilt as you grow older.

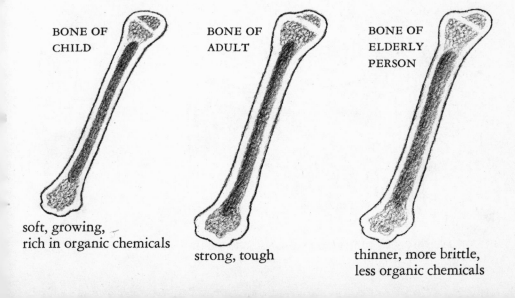

BONE OF CHILD

BONE OF ADULT

BONE OF ELDERLY PERSON

soft, growing, rich in organic chemicals

strong, tough

thinner, more brittle, less organic chemicals

The fresh bone is put down layer after layer, in the holes that have formed. New layers are built inside the older ones till the hole is almost filled. The only room that is left is for the tiny blood vessel at the center. When bone is cut across and examined under a microscope, the layer pattern can be seen.

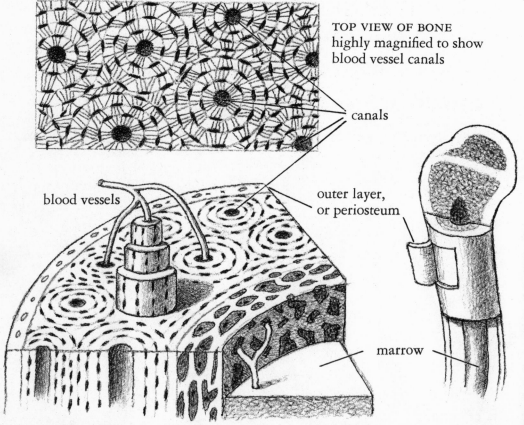

TOP VIEW OF BONE
highly magnified to show
blood vessel canals

canals

blood vessels

outer layer,
or periosteum

marrow

THREE-DIMENSIONAL DIAGRAM OF BONE STRUCTURE

Because of these changes as bone is replaced, bones actually can adjust to different conditions. An athlete's strong muscles pull, or put stress upon, his bones. So, as bone is rebuilt, it responds to the stress. It becomes heavier and stronger. The places where muscles are attached become larger. The more you use your skeleton in work or in play, the better the chances are that your bones will grow and rebuild normally—or become even stronger.

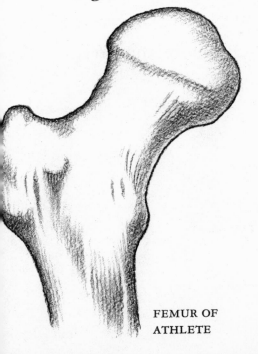

FEMUR OF
ATHLETE

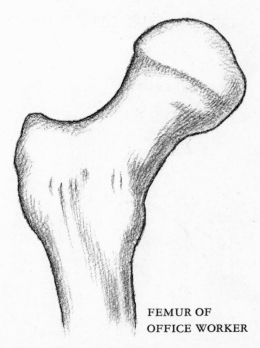

FEMUR OF
OFFICE WORKER

Bone cells also respond in an emergency, as when a bone is broken. Many more bone cells than usual appear at the break. In addition, some kinds of related cells change and take over the work of bone cells. Fresh bone is deposited heavily around the fracture, which the doctor has set in place and fastened with a cast. Sometimes a doctor will urge you to use a broken leg slightly. The extra stress on the fracture actually will speed up the repairs. The new bone around the fracture will form a callus of bone heavier and stronger than existed before the break.

KINDS OF FRACTURES

 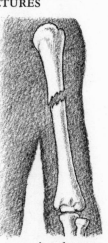  

greenstick   simple   compound   multiple

When you break a bone, the healing process starts almost at once. The doctor helps by setting the bone. He gets the broken ends in line and close together. A cast prevents any movement at the break. Once the cast is in place, the rest is up to you.

All the healing is done by microscopic cells. Soon after the break blood clots form (1) stopping the flow of blood from torn blood vessels. Then the osteoclast cells go to work (2) absorbing bone fragments and injured bone. At almost the same time osteoblast cells begin to deposit bone and tie the broken ends together (3). These cells increase in number and soon are building bone at a rapid rate. But the repair job may take several weeks, or longer. Finally the break is completely healed with an overgrowth of bone—a callus (4), which is actually thicker and stronger than the original bone.

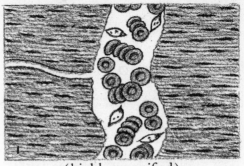

(highly magnified)

(highly magnified)

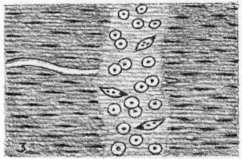

(highly magnified)

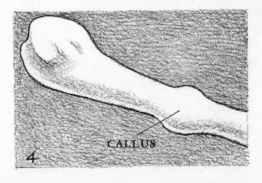

CALLUS

Almost as important as the bones themselves are the joints where one bone connects to another. A skeleton without joints would be as useless as a board, for its parts could not move separately. With joints you bend your arm, nod your head, or stand on your toes. At some joints, however, the motion is limited or there is no motion at all. The partly formed bones of a baby's skull move a bit and give enough so that there is no injury to its head or brain as the baby is born. But when the fontanels, or soft spots, seal, the connections between most bones of the skull and face no longer permit movement. These bones join along a zigzag crack, or suture. By the time a person grows old, the skull bones have grown across the sutures, which nearly disappear.

The backbone is also somewhat rigid. But in this column of bones there is always some movement. Bend from the hips, and you will feel that the joints of the backbone permit movement in nearly all directions. Still, at the very base of the backbone, where support is important, much less movement is possible. Here the bones fuse together.

Posture is the way we hold our bodies and use our skeletons. Some positions or postures aid health, and exercise often improves posture. No single kind of posture is the best, but it should make you feel good and help you do things more easily.

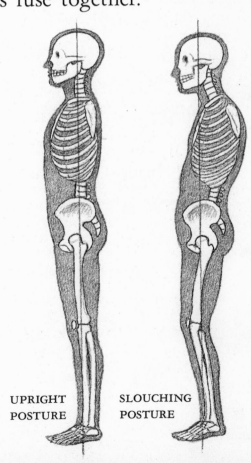

UPRIGHT POSTURE   SLOUCHING POSTURE

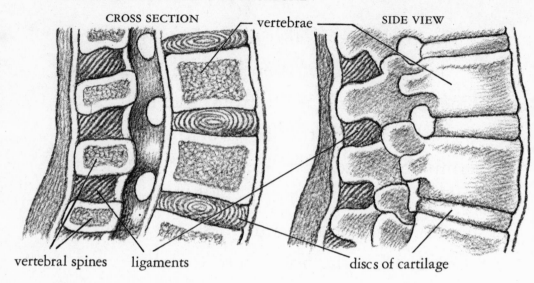

DISCS AND LIGAMENTS OF BACKBONE

CROSS SECTION — vertebrae — SIDE VIEW

vertebral spines   ligaments   discs of cartilage

The movement of your spine is limited because a disc of cartilage fits between the bones at each joint. These sandwiches of bone and cartilage that make up your backbone are bound together by tough fibers, or ligaments, that wrap around and between them. So while you can bend forward, backward, and sidewise, the movement is limited. The cartilage discs shrink with age. Thus old people may lose an inch or so in height.

Most joints, however, allow for free movements of different kinds. Best known are the ball-and-socket joints of your shoulders. They move in more directions than any other joints in your body. But no joint can turn in every direction because of the connections of blood vessels and nerves in it. Your hips

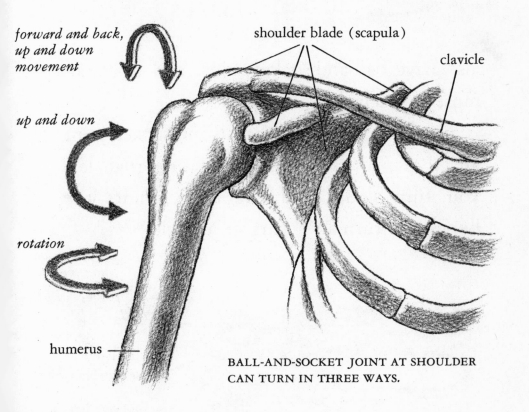

forward and back, up and down movement

up and down

rotation

shoulder blade (scapula)

clavicle

humerus

BALL-AND-SOCKET JOINT AT SHOULDER CAN TURN IN THREE WAYS.

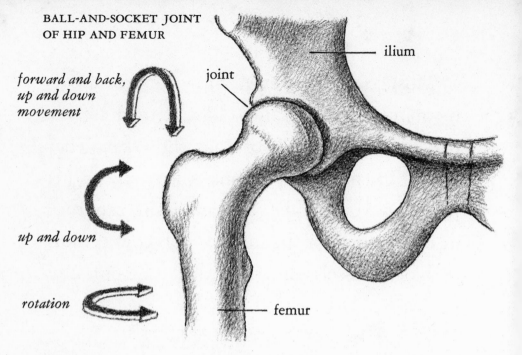

BALL-AND-SOCKET JOINT OF HIP AND FEMUR

forward and back, up and down movement

joint

ilium

up and down

rotation

femur

also have ball-and-socket joints and move almost as freely as your shoulders.

Not quite as free as a ball-and-socket joint are the pivot joints like the one that lets you turn your head. At these points the bones can turn in a part of a circle.

up and down movement

side to side movement

first vertebra (atlas)

second vertebra (axis)

OCCIPITAL BONE OF SKULL

Joints like those of the fingers permit back-and-forth movement only, like the hinge of a door. Your knees and ankle joints are also hinge joints. Other joints that permit the bones to move in two directions are the joints of your wrists and at the base of your thumbs. Still other joints, like those in the palm of your hand, allow only a very limited gliding movement. In all, there are six kinds of joints that move in some way, and two kinds that do not.

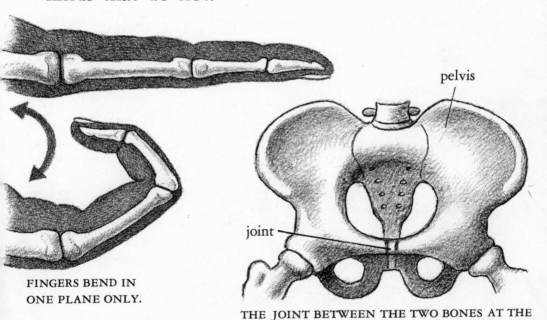

FINGERS BEND IN
ONE PLANE ONLY.

THE JOINT BETWEEN THE TWO BONES AT THE
FRONT OF THE PELVIS IS SLIGHTLY MOVEABLE.

A mechanic keeps all the moving parts of his machine well oiled so they turn easily. Joints that allow free movement are in a sense self-oiling. The two ends of the bone (in your knee, for example) fit together. Both are covered with smooth cartilage on top of which is a thin, tough membrane. This membrane releases a fluid that works like oil, cushioning the joint and helping it to move without rubbing. The two bones at the joint are bound together by tough ligaments, or cords. They stretch as the joint moves, but keep a firm grip on the two bones.

CROSS SECTION OF A KNEE JOINT WITH ITS FLUID

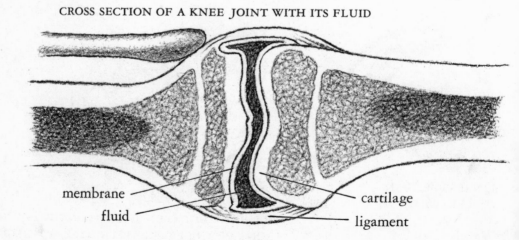

membrane

fluid

cartilage

ligament

If a joint is twisted or wrenched suddenly in an accident, the ligaments may be stretched or torn. This condition is called a sprain. The joint may swell and be difficult to use. If the wrench is very severe, the bone may be pulled out of contact with the joint or out of its socket. Then you have a dislocation. The doctor will work the bone back into the joint, and then relieve the pain with heat or medicines.

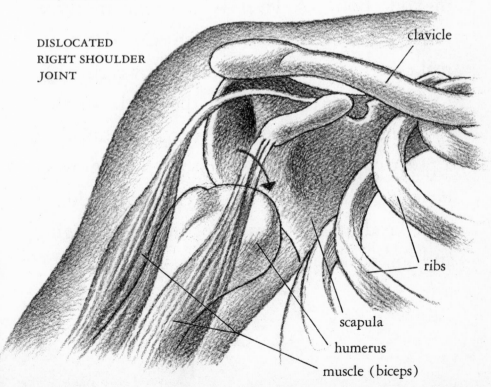

DISLOCATED
RIGHT SHOULDER
JOINT

clavicle

ribs

scapula

humerus

muscle (biceps)

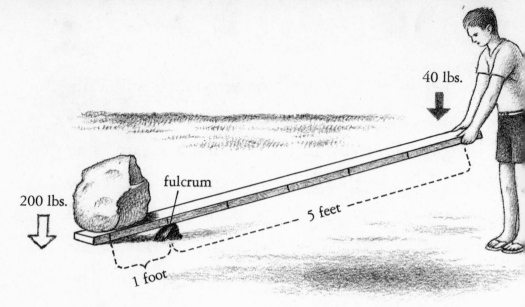

40 lbs.

fulcrum

200 lbs.

5 feet

1 foot

The bones, the joints, and the sets of muscles attached to them form systems of levers in your body. A lever is a simple machine that permits movement with less effort or makes it easier to lift heavier weights. A force must be used to do the work—in this case, the pull of muscles. There also must be a pivot or fulcrum on which the lever moves. Here are three types of levers: for nodding your head up and down, for lifting a weight, and for walking.

LEVERS IN YOUR BONES

When you nod your head,
your skull pivots
at the top of your backbone.

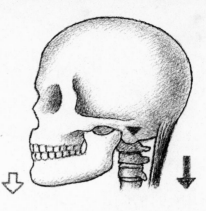

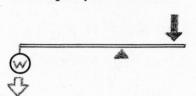

Lifting, throwing, and
picking things up use
your arms and fingers as levers.

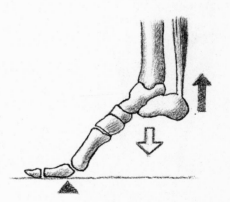

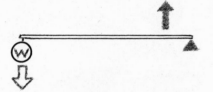

Walking, running, and kicking
use the lever action
of your feet and legs.

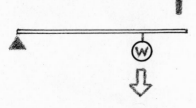

The study of bones takes in all backboned animals from fish to man. There is probably no bone smaller than the ear bones of a bee hummingbird, whose body is scarcely an inch long, or the rib of a guppy, a fish about the same length. The largest single bone is an upper arm bone of the huge brachiosaur dinosaur, dug up in Colorado. It was seven feet long and bigger than a football player. Equally

THERE ARE 7 BONES
IN THE LONG NECK
OF A GIRAFFE.

THERE ARE
14 BONES
IN THE
SHORT NECK
OF A SPARROW.

remarkable is the fact that a five-inch sparrow
has more bones in its short neck (14) than
an 18-foot giraffe has in its long one (7).

Usually we think of bone as slow growing,
since it takes 15 to 18 years for a person to

March   *June*

reach full height. But the antlers of a male deer, which are made of good solid bone, grow at a prodigious rate. Antlers begin as small bumps on the frontal bones of the deer's skull. As they grow so does the skin, or velvet, that covers the antler. The velvet provides food, calcium, and phosphorus through a rich network of blood vessels. Four to five months later the antlers are full grown. Those of a large elk or moose may spread six feet. Antlers of a deer make up two to four percent of the animal's weight.

stag with full spread of antlers

September

Soon after antlers are full grown, the velvet dies and the deer rubs it off against tree trunks. The antlers remain as bare dead bone. At the end of the spring mating season they, too, are shed. A new and perhaps larger set of antlers grows the next year. There is no record of any faster bone growth. How the deer can supply all this mineral matter from its food, through its blood supply, is not yet completely explained.

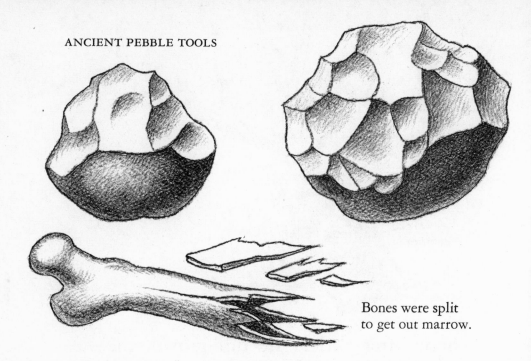

Bones were split
to get out marrow.

Long ago men learned that bone could be a useful material. Perhaps they first discovered that the fatty marrow of bone was a rich and delicate food. Together with some of the oldest human tools, crushed and broken bones have been found. Apparently the tools were used to get out the marrow. Some of these bones were human bones.

Today bones seldom are eaten. But a good

cook will tell you that a rich soup should always have a soupbone in it. Now most of the bones are cut out of meat before it is packaged and sold. Ground-up bones were once used for fertilizer because of the phosphorus in them. When millions of buffalo were killed on our Great Plains a century ago, the bones were gathered and sent to fertilizer factories. Furthermore, phosphate rock, which is mined for fertilizer in Florida, comes mainly from fossil bones.

FERTILIZERS BEFORE AND NOW

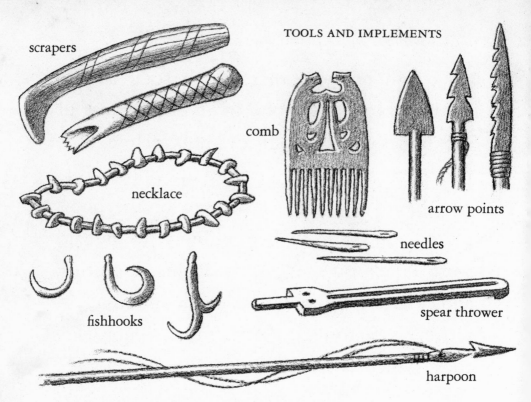

scrapers

comb

necklace

arrow points

needles

fishhooks

spear thrower

harpoon

Because bone is hard, tough, and can be polished, it was used widely in ancient times. Thousands of years ago, before man learned to work with metals, he had tools of bone. In caves and graves, archeologists have found bone needles, scrapers, knives, arrow and spear points, spear throwers, beads, and other ornaments.

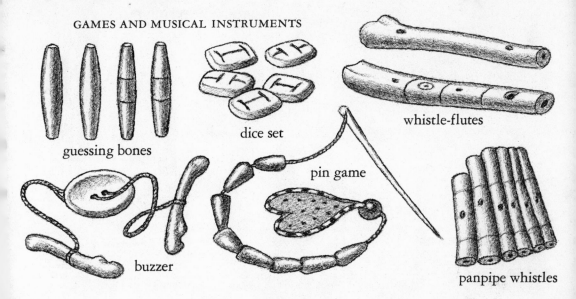

GAMES AND MUSICAL INSTRUMENTS

dice set

whistle-flutes

guessing bones

pin game

buzzer

panpipe whistles

In scattered places over the world, people have made whistles, flutes, rattles, and other musical instruments out of bone. Many beautiful carvings of bone have been found. They should not be confused with ivory, which is the tooth of an elephant or a walrus. Because polished bone is hard and smooth, it often was made into counters for games or into pieces for the games themselves. So you still hear people talking of "bones" when they mean dice or sometimes dominoes.

Bones last long after an animal or a person dies. So people once thought that the spirit of the animal or person remained in the bones. Indians of eastern Canada would never throw fishbones into their campfires. They knew that so doing would displease the fish spirits and fish would no longer come to their hooks and nets.

Our ancestors in Europe, just a few hundred years ago, also felt that bones had unusual power. The bones of a very good or very holy man often were preserved. A person who got a bit of such a bone felt that that the holiness of the man would protect him and his family. If the owner was rich, he kept the bone in a beautiful container of silver or of gold.

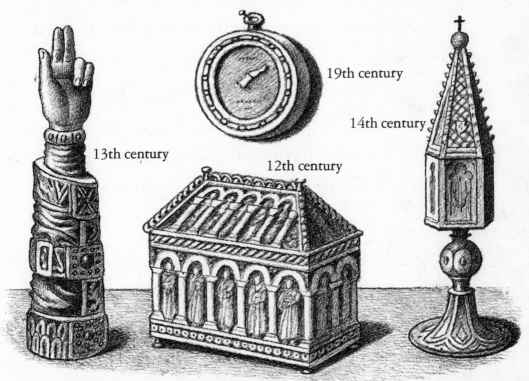

19th century

14th century

13th century

12th century

RELIQUARIES FOR SACRED BONES

Long ago people gathered up human and animal bones. At the right season they burned the bones in a big fire. Thus, they got rid of the spirits that lived in the bones, for spirits in common everyday bones might do harm to the living. Later these bone fires became bonfires, and we still light them outdoors for a victory or some other celebration. At Halloween, we have fun with bones, skeletons, and spirits in other ways.

When people work very hard, they sometimes say they are bone tired. This idea of
hard work going to the bone also may ac-
count for our saying we bone up when we
talk about studying hard for an examination.
With or without an exam, boning up on
bones is extremely important for us all.

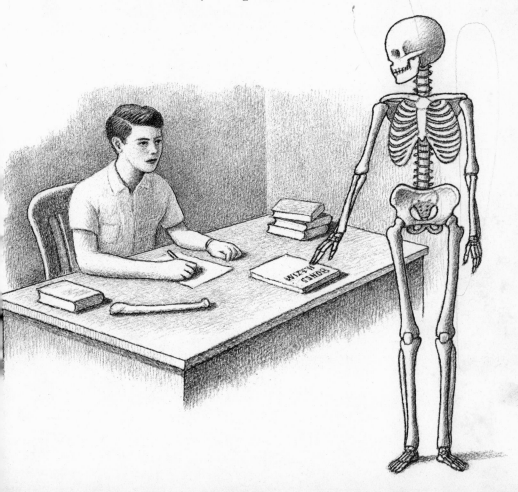

INDEX

Indicates illustrations